Thumb Basics

on Electric Bass by Jon org.

Amsco
London/New York/Sydney/Cologne

Exclusive Distributors:
Music Sales Limited
78 Newman Street, London W1P 3LA, England

Music Sales Corporation
24 East 22nd Street, New York, N.Y. 10010, USA

Music Sales Pty. Limited
27 Clarendon Street, Artarmon, Sydney, NSW 2064, Australia

© Copyright Day Eight Music Production, Sweden.
This edition © Copyright 1984 by
Amsco Publications
ISBN 0.7119.0503.7
Order No. AM36765

Cover designed by Mike Bell
Cover photography by Peter Wood
Translated by Jean-Cristophe Morrison

Music Sales complete catalogue lists thousands of
titles and is free from your local music book shop,
or direct from Music Sales Limited.
Please send 25p in stamps for postage to
Music Sales Limited, 78 Newman Street, London W1P 3LA.

Printed in England by
West Central Printing Co. Limited, London.

FOREWORD

This book is made for those of you who have played bass for some time and would like to learn "thumb-technique". The idea for this book arose from the many bassists I've met after gigs, thumb in air, asking: "How do you do that?!! I've always tried to show as much as possible, but in fifteen minutes you can do only so much. In any case I've finally finished the book — which is the first of its kind as far as I know — to satisfy all of you bass players who want to learn how to mishandle your basses and your thumbs at the same time.

The book consists of two parts. First comes instruction in the different techniques you must be able to command. Included in this part are some simple exercises on each basic technique. Next comes a practical section which combines the different techniques through a series of exercises (notated). If you have trouble reading notes I think the included record will be of some help. All of the exercises are recorded.

I've tried as much as possible to avoid bullshit in the text. This is an instruction book. That means there are no more words than necessary. Therefore, go through it several times carefully.

GOOD LUCK

Whichever instrument you play it is very important to have a relaxed hand. To get an ideal position for funk bass, completely relax the striking hand with the back of the hand outwards as shown in the photograph.

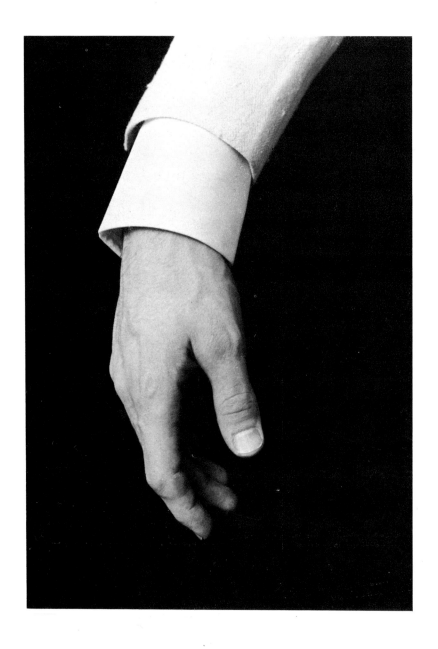

Striking with the thumb.

There are two places on the strings that are most effective when hit with the thumb. The first and easiest is at the end of the fingerboard. Hold your hand parallel with the strings, index finger approximately over the G-string and the thumb pointing straight up.

(From the basic hand position you move the striking hand over the fingerboard as shown in the photograph.

Strike the string with the small bone which protrudes from the side of the thumb (see photograph).

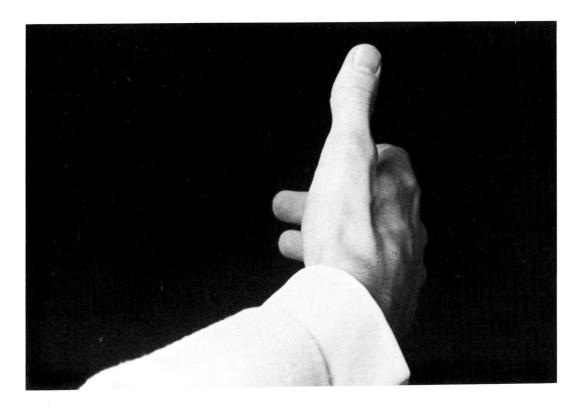

The actual striking motion is a twist of the wrist (it should feel as if the thumb falls by itself to the string). Attention!!! Do not use your arm.

The following series of photographs shows the striking movement step by step.

The following photographs show the striking motion from another angle.

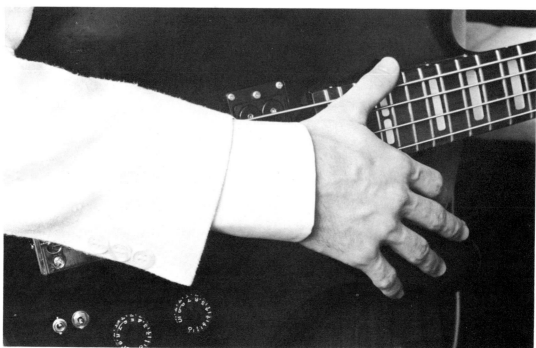

EXERCISE 1.   Strike the E-string slowly and carefully as shown previously. Try to make the string ring as much, and as long, as possible. Be sure to use the correct part of the thumb. This exercise gives control and speed so practise it often and hard even if it seems boring and meaningless.

The other place to strike is near the bridge. Hold your hand as shown in the photograph.

The striking motion is the same as before — a relaxed twist of the wrist, and using the same part of the thumb again.

The next series of photographs shows the striking motion step by step.

The same striking motion from another angle.

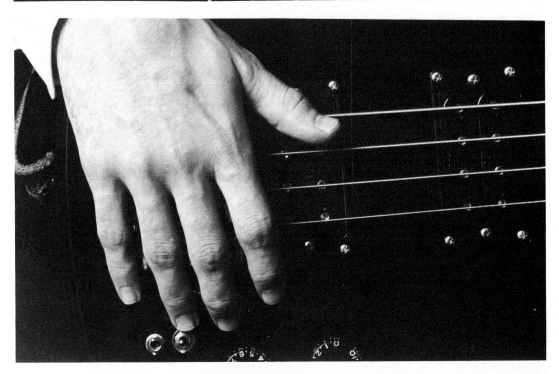

EXERCISE 2. Strike the E-string slowly and carefully as previously shown and try to make it ring as much, and as long, as possible. Attention!!! Strike right!!! Practise hard!!!

EXERCISE 3. As Exercise 1 but use E, A and D-strings.

EXERCISE 4. As Exercise 2 but use E, A and D-strings.

FINGERING HAND

Begin by holding it exactly the same as the striking hand.

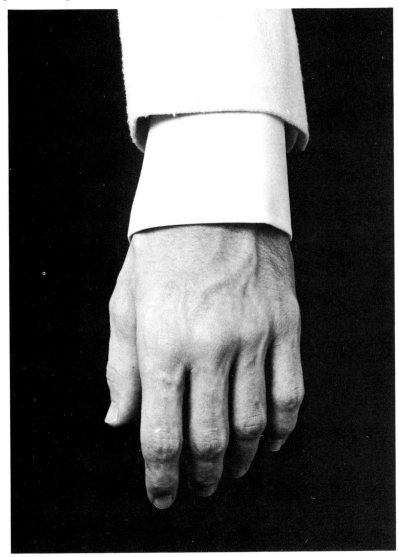

Then turn it upside down . . .

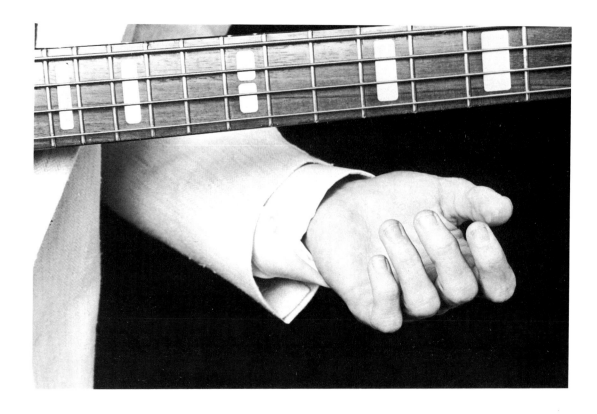

. . . and take hold of the neck without changing the hand position. You must play with the fingertips (see photograph).

Fingering hand from the front.

NOTE!!! Use your fingertips! No flat fingers on the fingerboard.

The thumb should lay about the middle of the underside of the neck.

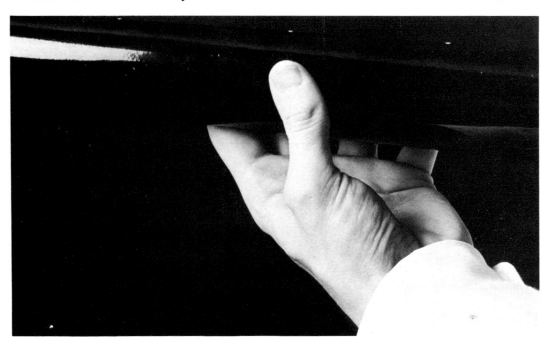

NOTE!!! Sometimes you must use flat fingers on the fingerboard (see photograph), but this should be considered exceptional.

POPPING TECHNIQUE

The other funk bass technique is to pull a string and slap it against the fingerboard. This technique has many names, but I've chosen to call it 'popping'.

Take a wide grip on the neck with much of the finger under the string as shown in the photograph.

At this point use only the index finger. Pull the string and release. The finger should glide off the string when you release it.

EXERCISE 5.   Take an E on the G-string and practise this technique. **Practise slowly!!** Make sure you get a good 'pop' when you release the string.

You can also 'pop' with the middle finger. But should you use both fingers in combination you must do it carefully because it strains the tendons in your hand quite a lot.

EXERCISE 6.   Take an E on the G-string and 'pop' it first with the index finger and then with the middle finger.
Absolutely not the other way round! because this strains your tendons. Practise slowly and methodically and be careful not to overwork the tendons in your hand.
NOTE!!! Try not to bend your index finger under the middle finger when you move it back to 'pop' again. Instead, move your whole hand.

You 'pop' most often with the G-string, but it also happens on the D-string and occasionally on the A-string. You rarely strike the G-string with the thumb.

HAMMER ON

A third form of playing is called "hammer on." This is when you use a finger of the fingering hand to strike the string down on to the fingerboard hard enough to produce a click and a tone. For example, on the A-string take a D and strike with your thumb. Then, (relatively quickly), strike your middle and ring fingers down to E on the same string. You get a short click and the string rings E (see photograph).

Strike the string with the thumb of the striking hand.

Hit the string with the middle and ring fingers of the fingering hand. NOTE! You shouldn't hit E with the middle finger, it should hit the D♯. It serves to add power to the ring finger.

19

When you want to hit an interval of one half step, you use only one finger. When you want a whole step interval you may use two fingers.

EXERCISE 7.   Take a C♯ on the A-string with the index finger. Strike the string with the thumb. Hit the middle finger down on D on the same string. Strike the D on the same string with the thumb and hit the ring and little fingers down on E on the same string (see photographs).

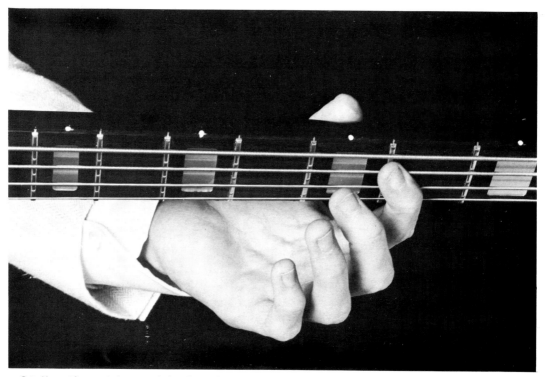

Strike the string with the thumb.

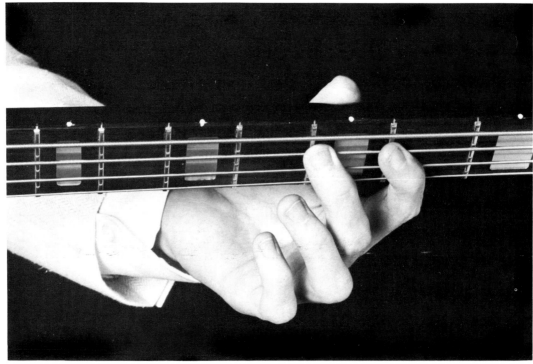

Hit the middle finger down and strike the string again with the thumb.

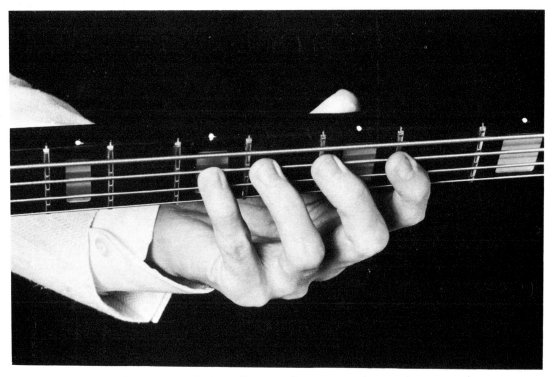

Hit the little finger and ring finger down on the string.

You can also use "hammer on" when you "pop". The technique is the same. The difference is that you pull, instead of strike, with the thumb.

EXERCISE 8.   Take a D on the G-string with the index finger. "Pop" it and hit the middle and ring fingers down on E on the same string. It should make a short click and E should ring.

HAMMER OFF

'Hammer off' is when you take, for example, an E on the A-string
with the ring finger and then strike with the thumb of the striking
hand, at the same time keeping the index finger down two frets
below (see photograph).

Then you **pull** the ring finger off the string hard enough to become
a "strike" for the D.

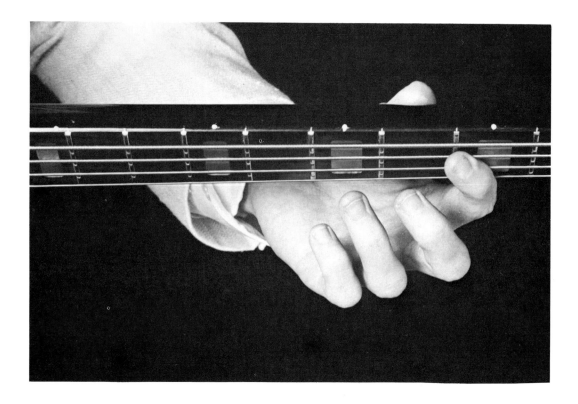

EXERCISE 9.   Practise the above technique.

Of course you can also use 'hammer off' when you "pop". The procedure is exactly the same. For example, you can take E on the G-string with the ring finger and "pop" it. At the same time, of course, you have the index finger placed on D two frets below, then pull the ring finger off the string so that the D rings.

EXERCISE 10.   Practise the above.

As when 'hammering off', you use one finger for a half tone interval and two fingers for a whole tone interval as in the case of 'hammering on'.

EXERCISE 11.   Take an E on the A-string with the little finger. At the same time keep the middle finger on D and the index finger on C♯. Rest the ring finger on D♯. Strike an E with the thumb. Pull the little finger away from the string **HARD** ('hammer off') and let the ring finger follow. (NOTE! The ring finger comes up at the same time as the little finger and has nothing to do with the tone produced). The D should ring. Strike the string again with the thumb, and 'hammer off' the middle finger so that C♯ rings.

EXERCISE 12.   Begin with Exercise 11 again. Then turn the
Exercise around and use 'hammer on' to come up. When you have
come to C♯ in Exercise 11, strike the C♯ again with the thumb,
hit down with the middle finger on D, strike the D again with the
thumb. Finally, hit the ring and little fingers on E (ring finger rests
on D♯ and not on the E, its purpose is to give a little extra power
to the "hit"). (See photographs).

Strike with the thumb.

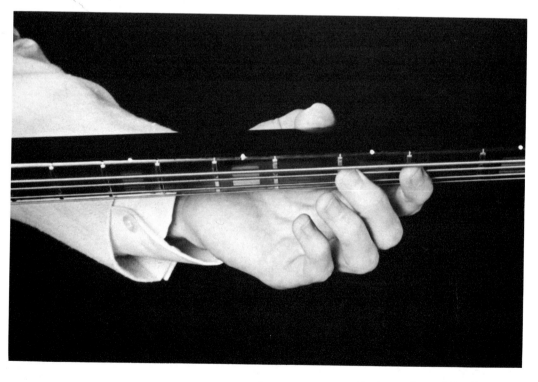

Pull off the little finger and ring finger and strike again with the
thumb.

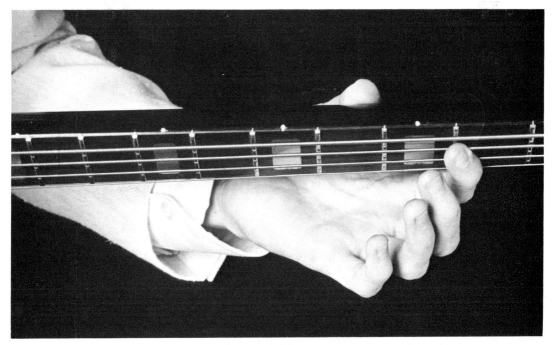

Pull off the middle finger and strike again with the thumb.

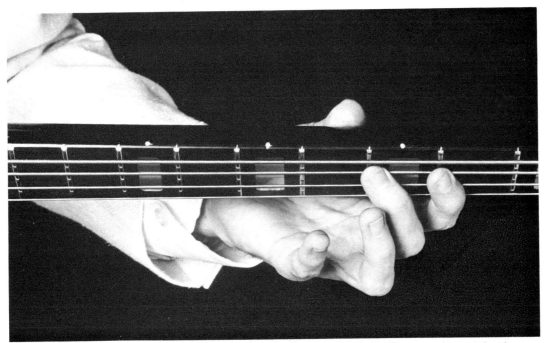

Hit the string down with the middle finger and strike again with the thumb.

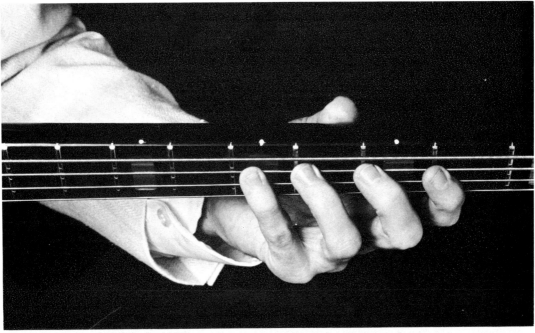

Hit the string down with the little finger and the ring finger.

EXERCISE 13.   This is a repetition of Exercise 11 but instead of striking with the thumb, you "pop". Take an E on the G-string with the little finger. Keep the middle finger on D and the index finger on C♯. Rest the ring finger on D♯. "Pop" the E and pull off the little finger and ring finger. The D rings. "Pop" the D and pull off the middle finger. The C♯ rings.

EXERCISE 14.   Begin with Exercise 13 again. Then turn the phrase around and use 'hammer on' to come up. When you have come down to C♯ you "pop" it again and hit down with the middle finger on D, "pop" it again and finally hit down with the ring and little finger on E. (NOTE!!! The ring finger has nothing to do with the tone produced). (See photographs.)

"Pop" the string.

Pull the ring finger and little finger off and "pop" it again.

Pull off the middle finger and "pop" it again.

Hit the string down with the middle finger and "pop" the string again.

Hit the string down with the little and ring fingers.

Exercises 13 and 14 are also excellent for practising coordination between the index and middle fingers of the striking hand in "popping". Alternate fingers each time you "pop". Always begin with the index finger. When you have "popped" once with both fingers, lower the whole hand so that the index finger finds its string without twisting under the middle finger (keep hand in position!). Be extremely careful that your hand is relaxed and not strained or wrongly positioned.

SCALES

The most common scales used in "thumb funk bass" are:

DORIAN

for Exercise E Dorian:

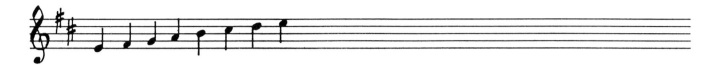

The Dorian scale consists of: a whole step, half step, whole step, whole step, whole step, half step, whole step.

MIXOLYDIAN

for Exercise E Mixolydian:

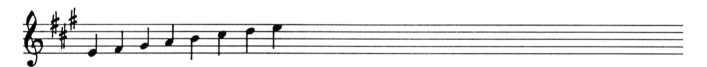

The Mixolydian scale consists of: a whole step, whole step, half step, whole step, whole step, half step, whole step.

and the BLUES SCALE

for Exercise E Blues scale:

The Blues scale consists of: one and half step, half step, half step, whole step, whole step, half step, whole step.

Of course you must consider the chord being played, but otherwise the most important notes for funk playing are the tonic, the major sixth and the minor seventh, which are found in all three of these scales.

DAMPED NOTES

Quite often the thumb and "popping" techniques are used with another technique that does not allow notes to ring. You damp the string with the fingering hand. I will indicate this with the following symbols:

Thumb Technique and Chord Progressions

If you want to use thumb technique for a certain chord progression you should look at it as another way of striking the strings, rather than as a special style although it is just that when you play modal funk. (Modal means you play around a particular chord and its scale all the time.) Similarly, you should consider when to use fingers or a plectrum, but strike the strings with the thumb or "pop" them instead. There are, of course, tunes where you blend modal funk and ordinary chord progressions.

EXERCISES

The following exercises should help you learn the techniques from the practical side. But you will also find phrases that can be useful in creating your own ideas.

KEY TO NOTATION

The finger which is used to strike or play the string is indicated below the note with the abbreviations:
T = Thumb
P = Index finger
L = Middle finger

'Hammer on' and 'hammer off' are indicated by a slur between the preceding note and the resulting note.
The string which is played is indicated below the note by a number:
G-string = 1
D-string = 2
A-string = 3
E-string = 4

EXERCISE 15

EXERCISE 16

EXERCISE 17

EXERCISE 18

EXERCISE 19

EXERCISE 20

EXERCISE 21

EXERCISE 22

T4 T3 T2   P2   T4 P2 T4 P2 T4 P2 T4 P2

EXERCISE 23

T4 T3 T3 P1 P1   P1   T4 T3 T3 P1 T3 P1 T3 P1
T4

EXERCISE 24

T4 T2 T2 P1 P1   P1   T4 P2 T4 P2 T4 P2 T4 P2
T4

EXERCISE 25

T4 T3 T3 P2 P2   T4   P2   T4 P2 T4 P2 T4 P2 T4 P2

EXERCISE 26

T4 P2 T3 T2 T2   T4   P2   T4 P2 T4 P2 T4 P2 P1 P1

EXERCISE 27

T4 P1 T3   T4   P1   T3 P1 T3 P1 T3 T3 P1 T3 T3 P1 T3

EXERCISE 28

T4 P1 T2 T4   P1   T4 P2 T4 P2 T4 T4 P2 T4 T4 P2 T4

EXERCISE 29

T4 P2 T2 T4　　P1　　T4 P2 T4 P2 T4 T4 P2 T4 T4 P2 T4

EXERCISE 30

T4 P1 T2 T4　　P2　　T4 P2 T4 P2 T4 T3 P1　T4 P2 T4

EXERCISE 31

T4 P2 T4 P2 T4 P2　　P2　T4　T4　P2　P2　T4　T4　P1

EXERCISE 32

T3 P1 T3 P1 T3 P1　　P1　　P1　T4 P1　　P1　　P1
　　　　　　　　　　　　T3　T4

EXERCISE 33

T4 P2 T4 P2 T4 P2　　P2　T4　P2　T3　P2　　T4
　　　　　　　　　　　T4

EXERCISE 34

T4 P2 T4 P2 T4 P2　　P2　T4　P1　P1　P1　　P2
　　　　　　　　　　　T4　　　　　　　　　　T4

EXERCISE 35 The following exercises concentrate on coordination
between the index and middle fingers of the striking hand.

P1　　P1　　T4　　T3 T3 P1　L1

34

EXERCISE 36

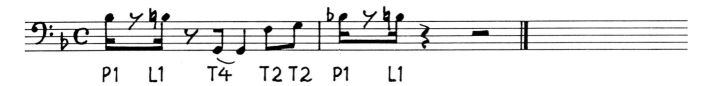

P1   L1   T4   T2 T2 P1   L1

EXERCISE 37

P2   L2   T4   T3 P2 P2   L2

EXERCISE 38

P2   L2   T4   T3 P2 P2   L2

EXERCISE 39 Here are two exercises that are a little longer. I have
put together extracts from the previous exercises to make a
complete phrase.

T4 T3 T3   P1   T4 T4   T4 T3 T3   P1

T3 P1 T3 P1 T3 P1 T3 P1   T4 T3 T3   P1   T4 P2
                                                        T 4

T4 T3 T3   P1   T3 P1   P1 T3 P1   P1
                              T3   T3

35

EPILOGUE

Remember that funk bass should be suggestive, quite repetitive, and with few variations. There should be pauses in your phrases. The heaviest funk bassist is the one who can stand on one note in every second measure and make it swing like hell. Work up a good technique but use sparingly. Remember that funk is aggressive, striving music and play your asses off!!!

GOOD LUCK